HOW TO SURVIVE THE COLLAPSE OF YOUR SOCIETY.

By SGT. C. Barnard

Chapter

Better to have it and not need it than need it and not have it- words to live by

CHAPTER 1
REASONS TO BE PREPARED.

Throughout the world, history has shown us that societies collapse. Since the dawn of time events have occurred that have caused humans to run for their lives and start over with little to no resources. Be it a Natural Disaster, Famine, War, Civil unrest, or a National/ Global Financial crisis. While we all would like to believe that none of these events will happen to us history has proven that at the very least a natural disaster will happen during our lifetime. Fortunately Natural Disasters are usually confined to a small area and it is possible to escape with a few belongings to help establish yourself or sustain you and your family until you return back home.

Famine, War, Civil unrest and Financial Crisis are not so easily resolved. Let's examine Famine first because each of the other triggers causes Famine. Most people look at famine as a loss of crops due to soil erosion or drought but famine is basically defined as a scarcity of food resulting in extreme hunger or starvation. A war will limit resources for civilians and be redirected to the fighting force; a natural disaster will put a lot of people trying to survive on what they have until rescuers arrive with needed Supplies. Civil unrest will create a supply and demand situation where prices could soar beyond reason. Financial crises could cause job loss, homelessness, and eliminate all ability to acquire the money to feed your family.

As we saw as recently as the 2005 Hurricane Katrina disaster and the collapse of the Levee shortly thereafter resulted in 80 percent of the city flooded, rendering most of the population stranded in deplorable conditions with no way out. While the rest of the country was not experiencing famine the citizens of New Orleans were. It is necessary to be prepared because you just never know when you may be forced to sit and wait for someone to rescue you or flee to a safer area, and one thing that is a certainty is that it will happen at the most inconvenient time possible.

For those that could not flee after Hurricane Katrina, most of the resources available throughout the city were under water, or were blocked by flowing water and debris. This required people to scrounge for any food they could find, with no way to leave the spot they had been stranded in some of which was on a rooftop or the second floor of their house. Since most kitchens are located on the ground floor all of the food in the home was below water.

Most of the city's citizens struggled with the uncertainty and stress of not knowing how or even what to do. Resulting in a lot of civil unrest. People were arming themselves against looters. The military and FEMA were overwhelmed with the magnitude of victims and no place to put them. This caused strains on tempers and enabled a certain amount of lawlessness to capture the city.

Very Similar situations occurred in 2017 when eastern Texas was destroyed when Hurricane Harvey struck. News report after news report showed videos and pictures of thousands rendered homeless and barely able to navigate their way out of flowing waters. Luckily in Texas the state rallied together and people poured in to help but that was a temporary band aid because there was still the problem of where to place the now homeless thousands of families.

In times of war and civil unrest businesses close and become targets for looters, so having supplies on hand before this happens is important. Police become overwhelmed and can not be everywhere to maintain order. As we saw in the recent riots stores were looted and burned. People were forced to barricade their homes and wait for the angry mobs to disperse before they could safely travel for supplies

As we have seen the Color of your skin and the way you dress can make you a target as well. African Americans are targets if their appearance can be stereotyped as thuggish, sad but true. European Americans can be targets if they seem wealthy, or some can be stereotyped as a redneck. Hispanics can become targets if they speak with a thick accent and therefore stereotyped as being in the country illegally. It is a sad world that we live in and that a growing part of our population views other races with distrust but knowing how other races perceive you can help you blend in and prepare for those scenarios.

Some important things to think about and questions to ask yourself before the disaster happens.

1. How will I notify the rescuers that I need help?

2. Do I have a light source for signaling that can stay charged for long periods of time without batteries or electricity.

3. How will I keep dry, warm and fed?

4. How will I provide for those with me? Small children, Elderly, Handicapped?

5. Where is the safest place that I can get to?

6. What should I bring with me if I have to wait for an extended period of time before I can return home?

7. How will I protect myself and loved ones from other people?

8. What Survival Skills do I have?

9. What medical emergency can I provide assistance with.

10. Do I have an emergency Medical kit that can handle a variety of medical situations. Such as Burns, Cuts, Diarrhea, Broken Limbs, fever, even a simple headache.

WAR, just the thought of it can cause pictures to appear in your mind, Pictures from some book, action movie or documentary, even possibly a memory from a personal experience. One thing that is consistent about war is that supplies are harder to get and cities are targets. The Civil War, Pearl Harbor, 9-11 showed us that even America is not exempt from attack, even from our own countrymen. The riots that we periodically experience in cities across this nation can attest to the need to be prepared for many different scenarios.

Let's examine things that happen when a war breaks out. First someone attacks someone else usually on a large scale. With the Civil War confederate forces attacked Fort Sumter, in Pearl Harbor the Japanese attacked the Naval base in Hawaii. On 9/11 terrorist hijacked planes and flew them into and destroyed the World Trade Center's Twin Towers in New York City, damaged the Pentagon (the US Military Headquarters) and unsuccessfully attempted to fly the fourth plane into the White House.

During WWII there was a global shortage of Gas, Blood, Tires, Sugar, Flour, Medicine, and about anything else you would need or want. Most resources and factories were converted to help with the war effort. Leaving most private citizens to ration and figure out by themselves how to provide for their needs

Financial Crisis means recession or the dreaded depression. As we know the depression of the 1930s sent people plummeting to their death, and created multitudes of homeless families. Many companies went under and millions of people were left to figure out a way to survive with no job, no money and no home. The rest of the people that were fortunate enough to have money or resources such as a farm or a skill in demand were still barely getting by.

In   2008, many stores shut their doors causing many people to become unemployed while the country was experiencing some of the highest gas prices we have ever experienced, because of this many of these families were forced out of their homes and forced to move in with other family members or homeless shelters. Some are still there today. This is why it is crucial to be prepared for things beyond your control. This is why it is always good to have a plan for everything that could go wrong.

As I have explained at some point in your life disaster will strike and how prepared will you be? I have put together an emergency kit to help get you started thinking about what you will need.

Prepare for the Worst Hope for the Best! - words of wisdom

CHAPTER 2
PREPARING FOR COLLAPSE

The first thing to do when preparing for a collapse is to buy a backpack with outside pockets and is waterproof and has a strap to evenly distribute weight with wheels and handles for each person in your household. Fill it with the necessities listed and forget about it. Attach a collapsible dolly to the backpack you can use this to gather wood, water or anything else even pull tired children.

Keep one or two of these Packs in your car and additional ones in your home. Always keep extra clothing, water and a solar battery charger in your vehicle as well. You need to think about things you can't live without. For example, are you a smoker or a drinker? How many days can you go without having these things before becoming irritable? Do you want to be going through withdrawal in the middle of a crisis? Tensions will be high and it will not help if there is a stimulus that you can not remain calm without.

You can save yourself and those in your family by

beginning to wean yourself off slowly now. Yes, I know you are saying don't you think if I could do that I would. I completely understand that statement. So what does that leave us with then? Actually a few things include the stimuli that you can't function calmly without into your survival plan, buying some tobacco plants and learning how to dry and make your own chew, dip, cigarettes, cigars. Buy a rechargeable cigarette and put it in your bag. Make sure if you go "the grow your own" route that you have necessary supplies like rolling papers, a dehydrator, and have done a soil test on land that you will be growing on.

If Alcohol is your stimuli then you should include that in the pack as well in a bubble wrapped container and then placed in a zip locked bag so you don't damage other supplies if the container was to break) Maybe removing it from the original container to a more durable container would be worth exploring. Once you get to your location you can make your own. There are lots of internet videos showing how to make your own brews and wine. Create a grapevine at your bug out location to help start your process. I will cover that more in chapter 5.

One thing most of us forget about is our dependence on Caffeine, What happens to you when you are going through caffeine withdrawal? Are you irritable and Tired? Do you get a headache? I know I do. So how can we reduce these Problems? There are caffeine pills, individual coffee and tea packets. You can even buy syrup and a carbonator to make your own soda. It may be of the generic varieties but can help and can be stored at your bug out location.

Things to put in each backpack:

- Manual Winding flashlight (Wal-Mart, and Home Depot both sell them for around $7)
- Sheet and Thick blanket (put in a space saver bag.)
- Three changes of clothes (both winter and summer also put in space saver bag)
- Plastic jar of chicken and Beef Bullion (can be bought at any grocery store)
- A bar of antibacterial soap (put in ziplock bag)
- Toothbrush and paste (put in ziplock bag)
- Wet weather Poncho woodland color(this can also be used as a shelter)
- Large box of matches(put in ziplock bag)
- Three Self insulating blankets (these are sold everywhere for about $2 and come in a small bag put one in outside pocket)
- Cup and Bowl (Plastic, or metal)
- Fork, spoon, and a good Pocket Knife.
- Tube of anti bacterial ointment and diaper rash cream (put in ziplock bag).
- Small mirror (for signaling and checking area before moving put in outside pocket)
- MRE (Meal ready to eat) most army surplus stores sell these)
- Fishing line and 5 hooks and small net
- Two 40-gallon trash bags (need to be construction grade; these can be used with a blanket for a sleeping bag. Not for small children for them buy child sleeping bag (put in space saver bag)
- Hatchet with guard over blade and collapsible shovel

- 100 foot nylon cord/ rope and variety pack of bungee cords
- Spool of thread and pack of needles
- Two large bottles of water.
- Good slingshot. (silent and can be used to get small bird for food)
- Knife with six inch blade. 1000 rounds of Ammo for weapons you have.
- Bottle of water sterilizing tablets(put in ziplock bag)
- Scarf, hat and gloves (put in ziplock bag)
- Mothballs. (to keep bugs away)
- Foot powder and baby powder (ziplock bag)
- Bottle of pain relief medicine, allergies/cold medicine, and multivitamins.
- Pair of leather boots (one size too big for children.)
- Wet wipes
- Salt (needed to prevent dehydration)
- Map and compass (in outside pocket with routes established)
- Large Roll of toilet paper(put in ziplock bag)
- .Small radio with charging handle (or if cannot find one with batteries will do with headphones to prevent detection)
- Rechargeable batteries and solar charger (solar light tops are mini chargers)
- Dehydrated fruit and vegetables (zip lock bag)
- Large bag of pinto beans. (small bag of flour to bake for mold for penicillin)
- variety of seeds (to be used when you get to safe zone)
- Any medication needed (2 week supply)
- Air mattress (can use kind for pools with repair kit)
- Journal and pack of pencils with sharpener (to record vital information on surroundings put in zip-

lock bag in outside pocket)
- .Insect repellent lotion, Sunscreen, lip balm
- Duct tape and electrical tape
- Small camping pot (wrap in towel to prevent noise)
- Canteen (fill before leaving or soon as possible)
- Small solar charger (this can be bought online for $30. This can be used to charge anything that runs off a battery. Buy what you can afford it will come in handy many different ways)
- Five pairs of socks and underwear (put in ziplock bag and outside pocket)
- Windbreaker/lightweight jacket
- Coat (thin but warm try to buy one that is fleece and will compress down if you can get fleece pants as well DO you will need them)
- Toy for child(something small)survival book for adults
- Three tubes of glue/ super glue (can be used to close a wound and to repair items
  - Stimuli you can't live without

By putting the same items in each backpack this will reduce the chances of losing all emergency supplies. If it is going to take a while to get to the rally point you will need more supplies than are contained in one backpack. Remember that a trip that under normal circumstances may take an hour could take several hours or days depending on threat level both foreign and domestic.

Once this is complete, you are ready to prepare routes to get to a safe area. Talk to family and friends that you can trust about banding together and you can count on to pull their weight about a rally point. Pick one in each direction with established guidelines for going to each one. Consider these questions when deciding which site is best. What direction is the threat coming from? What is a central point for each person/group and how long to wait before leaving the rally point. What is the cover and concealment advantage of rally point?

Once this is complete, you are ready to prepare routes to get to a safe area. Talk to family and friends that you can trust about banding together and you can count on to pull their weight about a rally point. Pick one in each direction with established guidelines for going to each one. Consider these questions when deciding which site is best. What direction is the threat coming from? What is a central point for each person/group and how long to wait before leaving the rally point. What is the cover and concealment advantage of rally points?

Try to pick low populated spots that are off main roads and can be walked to if gas or traffic is a problem. If you have family/friends that live in a low population area near woods pick the one that has the best defendable location (On top of a hill, fenced in, sits back off road, and is not easily spotted because of trees or other natural landmarks. Do not share where your route or rally point is with anyone outside your groups.

Prior to the collapse, store additional survival items at rally points in a place that is not obvious. A good place would be down a capped well, buy a plastic tub with a lid, fill it up with non perishable food, seal it with duct tape and bury it in the yard where its view is concealed by a tree, briar patch or building. Then put something over that looks as if it belongs there (a lawn mower, rock pile, wood, or anything that makes it look normal and will conceal you accessing it if someone is passing by).

Each group should make a survival package at the rally point. This should be buried in a separate location. Designate general areas for each group but do not give specific locations this will help keep each party honest in a time of stress. This will also provide a variety of supplies.

Each group should put serious thought into what they can't live without food, clothing, medicine, building material, ammo, seeds, child needs like cloth diapers. Powdered formula and vitamins. Sterile water. Comfort items are not to be put in the survival kit. Hard candy can be included in a small quantity for a special treat much later but should be weighed against its value versus the area it will take up forcing something more important to be left out.

Try to communicate with all parties while on route via cell phones if lines still work or walkie-talkies if you have them. Some reasonably priced ones with 20-mile range can be bought for $20. Establish what channel you will use, write it on the first page of the journal, establish code words that are easy to remember.

Examples are: if you have three families trying to meet at rally point

Family one could be (use the street name the family lives on don't use person's name if possible)

Pine 1-1 for father

Pine 1-2 for mother

Pine 1-3 for oldest child

Continue down the line for each other member 1-4 thru 1-9.

Do the same for family two and three except they would be:

Walnut 2-1 father

Walnut 2-2 mother

Story 3-1 father

Story 3-2.

And so on for each family member.

Also, Pick words for location checks that have nothing to do with actual location but are an established name for a predestined landmark.

A scenario would be each family is meeting at grandma's house on the hill. Each group lives 15 miles away in a different direction. Each party has four established landmarks that have been shared with the other groups on the route they will be taking.

Pine 1-1 radios Walnut 2-1 to see where they are and Walnut 2-1 replies at the zoo watching the Monkeys (which actually means they are passing a Mall 3 miles from their house stopped because of traffic) Pine one replies: have fun buy a story book for me.

This lets 2-1 know the message has been received and that the third group is not there yet either and that they have not established contact. If contact with 3-1 has been made 1-1, could say have fun and laugh saying "I'll have to tell you a funny story later about our trip to the museum" (which translates to the location of 3-1.)

This also gives story 3-1 a chance to give their location if they are listening or in trouble. Communication is very important and needs to be practiced and memorized by each person in the group. If small children are involved, establish procedures for their safety along the route if adults become unable to continue so other groups can adjust routes to assist and get them to safety. Pick many places that they can be concealed and safe until they can be gotten to. Have code names for those as well.

What if you don't have any place to go? This is where planning comes into play. I have traveled to every state in this country and each of those states I have found cheap land for sale. Rule of thumb the further you are away from a large city the cheaper the land. While this is sad that property values are low in outlying areas, it is a good thing when looking for a cheap bug out location. As you can guess the more remote the better.

Spending a few thousand dollars now to acquire an acre in some remote part of the state, could keep your family safe in the future. Plus, it gives you a weekend getaway in the meantime. Spending time at that location prior to disaster will allow time to bring necessary supplies in so you are not starting from scratch. It will give you time to build a structure, or comb the free section of classified ads to acquire one.

One thing I have noticed is that hilltops are cheap. Due to the Cost of paving a road/driveway up to them most people do not want the hassle. But this is great in times of crisis because it provides high ground, seclusion, Visibility of surrounding area, and greater wind volume (great for a small wind Generator), it also will help in a flooding situation.

It also helps keep people away, people are lazy and would rather not have to climb a hill to fight and still have to climb back down. Most crime happens because of ease and opportunity. The harder it is to accomplish the less likely to be bothered. But that doesn't mean you shouldn't be prepared for the more stubborn criminals.

Always remember desperate people do desperate things. As Teddy Roosevelt said walk softly but carry a big stick. As former Secretary of Defence General Mattis said "Be polite but have a plan to kill everyone in the room". Both statements are vital to you and your families survival.

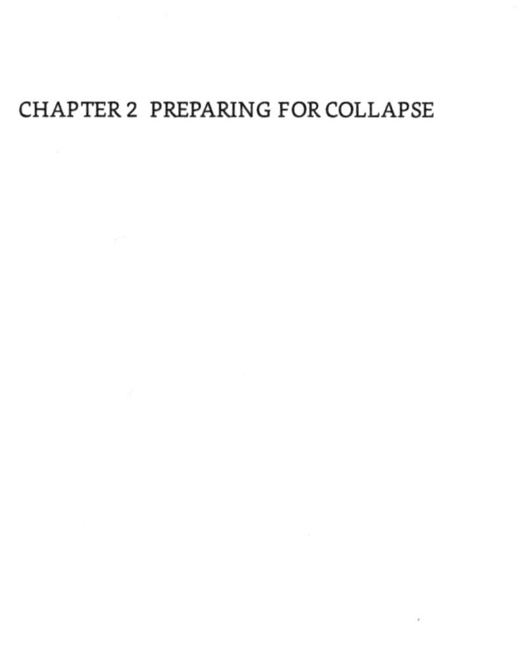

Always find the Backway and have a route of escape- Words of wisdom

CHAPTER 3: MOVEMENT DAY

While each group is moving to the rally point avoid heavily congested areas these are targets for the threat to attack and area's that mass hysteria is probably happening and is potentially more dangerous that the actual threat. Most people will not be prepared and will want to take what you have so be prepared to protect your group and belongings.

Some simple lightweight, not lethal, weapons are a stun gun, a tied sock filled with packed sand, and a bamboo stick/braided thin limbs of a bush (this stings and will help bring them to senses or move to an easier target.) A Baseball bat(all you walking dead fans know how effective it can be) a hammer, even a small one can be an effective weapon. A roll of pennies taped to the palm of a glove can give more power to your punch.

More lethal weapons that can be secured to you and not easily taken are a shotgun or rifle. Weapons should be loaded and ready to fire but placed on safe to prevent accidental discharge. Pistols are good to have and can be easily concealed. But, need to be secured to you by a holster with cord that can be attached to the weapon handle.

If you have a problem with guns or for whatever

reason cannot have one. There are other ways to protect your family. Move at night in a path that is less traveled. But odds are you will at some point need a way to defend you and yours. As much as we would like to live in a world where everyone is nice and cares about the safety of everyone else. The reaility is the human race has not evolved that far. We are still barely removed from our caveman days and still tend to lash out at one another in times of stress.

Below is a quick guide to use as a resource for Evacuation.

EVACUATION GUIDELINES

- Keep a full tank of gas in your car if an evacuation seems likely. But always keep a Gas can full of at least 5-10 gallons just in case it is one of those days you forgot to fill up. Don't forget that most of us have lawn mowers and other gas using yard equipment and can be used in an emergency. Gas stations may be closed during emergencies and unable to pump gas during power outages. Plan to take one car per family to reduce congestion and delay.
- Make transportation arrangements with friends or your local government if you do not own a car. Try to find an all terrain Bicycle cheap and outfit it to carry supplies
- Listen to a battery-powered radio and follow local evacuation instructions. Avoid crowded areas. Back roads tend to be less crowded than main roads
- Gather your family and go if you are instructed to evacuate immediately.
- Leave early enough to avoid being trapped by severe weather
- Follow recommended evacuation routes. Do not take shortcuts; they may be blocked.

- Be alert for washed-out roads and bridges. Do not drive into flooded areas.
- Stay away from downed power lines

IF TIME PERMITS:

- Gather your disaster supplies kit. Always try to have an additional disaster kit that is left in your Vehicle/s because you may not be home when disaster hits.
- Wear sturdy shoes and clothing that provides some protection, such as long pants, long-sleeved shirts, and a cap. Add a reflective vest if you are not worried about attack i.e. Natural Disaster
- Secure your home: Close and lock doors and windows. Board up if possible. Unplug electrical equipment, such as radios, televisions, small appliances. Leave freezers and refrigerators plugged in unless there is a risk of flooding.
- Let others that you love and trust know where you are going.
- Make sure that you establish a way to communicate with loved ones that will not be traveling with you so worry about loved ones will not add stress to an already stressful situation.

Make sure everyone in your group knows how to watch for threats. Now is not the time to be staring at a phone or handheld game. Don't forget your pet. A pet can provide a calming effect on small children. Dogs can keep people at bay for fear of being bitten.

Understand that everyone around you is stressed and scared and this makes them dangerous. People you see and interact with every day can become your worst enemy if they become desperate enough. Humans are by nature selfish and self centered. We are a species that has been bred to take what we want by any means necessary. As much as we try to claim that we are more civilized than that, the simple truth is we are not.

Try to dress as comfortably as possible, no need to be fashionable. Remember you will need to possibly wear the same clothes and shoes for more than one day. You may also need to run or walk a great distance across rough terrain in them.

Home is where the story begins what do you want your story to be?- words of wisdom

CHAPTER 4 - FORTIFYING YOUR HOME/RALLY POINT

Some of us want to stay in our home no matter what happens. If that is the choice you have made then there are steps you need to take to make that possible for as long as possible. First you need to evaluate the stability and safety of your home. Some questions to ask yourself are.

1. If a flood happens can I get to high ground/second floor?

2. Can my home structurally withstand water, weapons, fire, blasts?

3. How difficult will it be to make it more structurally sound?

4. Do I have strong locks that make it difficult for predators to get through?

5. Can I trust my neighbors?

6. How rational is it for me and my family to stay in this location?

7. Is it easy for help to get to me?

8. Can I sustain my family safely in this location?

After you have answered these questions and have made the decision to remain in your home here are some steps you can do to prepare for various perils as per the fema website. I will expand further after their suggestions if a flood happens

Items to have on hand in case of a flood

1. sandbags

2, shovel

3. Plank boards

4. Flotation device. I.e raft. Canoe, child floats, life vests,

5 tarp

6. Rubber boots

7. Waders

8. Waterproof matches

9. Dry wood

10. Fire pit placed at a higher elevation to cook and boil water.

To protect your family when a flood is predicted do the following: If there are ways to leave before it arrives always do so. In a bug out situation rescue probably will not be available and you will be forced to rescue yourself and loved ones again. Knowing where high ground is and a plan to get there is paramount.

That is why it is a good Idea to have a flotation vest for each person in your group. Even the very simple arm bands that we see little kids wearing poolside can be an effective aid in a flood, We all see several variations of flotation devices every summer buy a few inflatable air mats, these can also be used as beds that can be easily transported and stored until needed. Be sure to pick up repair kits for each one as well.

Buy a Boat of some sort, they have several inflatable canoes for under $100.00 and some that can hold 5 people for about $140.00 online. There is also the home made raft. When I was a little girl my dad told me a story about how they used a door as a raft when they went through a flood. Explore all possibilities for floatability and durability. Remember there will be a lot of debri that can damage your chosen device.

Always research your bug out location to see if you are in a floodplain. If so, look for a better location if possible. If it is not possible then trenching around the area and building the area up to a higher elevation can help this can be accomplished by hauling in sand and gravel. Putting bricks under the foundation of bugout dwelling and raising up 3 feet minimum. You can check the local planning and zoning offices to find out the floodplain status of bug-out location.

During and after a flood resources are limited. Some things that are vital to survival are water, and the ability to be dry and warm. Filling Sandbags will help keep water away from your home. Creating a plank system on top of the sandbags, you can have a dry way to move about your area until help arrives or the water recedes.

Yo need to understand that water will most likely be contaminated and you will need to boil your water. Depending on the extent of flooding you may be without power. If so you will need a way to boil your water. That is why you will need some dry wood and a fire pit to use for this purpose and it can be used in the absence of a grill to cook your food.

Staying warm and dry is important because getting sick with even a cold can become deadly in a bug-out situation. If we look back through history we can see how floods and the illnesses associated have had lasting effects even after the water has receded. The diseases and contamination they have left behind such as coloria, typhoid, hepatitis and several other infections caused by a simple scratch that can be infected by non boiled water touching a break in the skin.

Since doctor prescribed antibiotic meds and creams may not be available in a timely manner it is always a good Idea visit your local health food store and research natural antibiotics and always have some antibacterial cream on hand. Also take the time to know what is the true expiration date for your medicine.

The reason I say this is because when I was in the Army I was in charge of ordering and maintaining disaster readiness supplies and I was informed that the expiration date on medicine was not always the actual date and I had a book that detailed the actual date that was sometimes several years later. So do your research. Knowledge is power. Of course as i am sure you know anything that requires refrigeration does not have an extended shelf life outside of refrigeration. And should be tossed out for safety.

Explosions

Items needed for explosions

. 1. Boards

2. Tape

3. Tarps

4. First aid kit.

5. A first aid manual

6 . an emergency radio

7. Hammer

8. Nails.

9. Zip ties

10. A solar charger

11. A bandana or mask

12. Flashlight

Terrorists have frequently used explosive devices as one of their most common weapons. Terrorists do not have to look far to find out how to make explosive devices; the information is readily available in books and other information sources. The materials needed for an explosive device can be found in many places including variety, hardware, and auto supply stores. Explosive devices are highly portable using vehicles and humans as a means of transport. They are easily detonated from remote locations or by suicide bombers.

Conventional bombs have been used to damage and destroy financial, political, social, and religious institutions. Attacks have occurred in public places and on city streets with thousands of people around the world injured and killed. I want to take a minute and share with you some information I picked up as a volunteer in my area from my county health office that had a large selection of books published by fema. I asked and was informed this is info in the public domain and was okay to share in my book. So here is the expert's guidance for explosions.

The Experts from FEMA State the following.

During an Explosion
If there is an explosion, you should:

- Get under a sturdy table or desk if things are falling around you. When they stop falling, leave quickly, watching for obviously weakened floors and stairways. As you exit from the building, be especially watchful of falling debris.

- Leave the building as quickly as possible. Do not stop to retrieve personal possessions or make phone calls.

- Do not use elevators.

Once you are out:

- Do not stand in front of windows, glass doors, or other potentially hazardous areas.

- Move away from sidewalks or streets to be used by emergency officials or others still exiting the building.

If you are trapped in debris:

- If possible, use a flashlight to signal your location to rescuers.

- Avoid unnecessary movement so you don't kick up dust.

- Cover your nose and mouth with anything you have on hand. (Dense-weave cotton material can act as a good filter. Try to breathe through the material.)

- Tap on a pipe or wall so rescuers can hear where you are.

- If possible, use a whistle to signal rescuers.

- Shout only as a last resort. Shouting can cause a person to inhale dangerous amounts of dust.

I pray daily this never happens but if it does the experts at FEMA suggest doing the following

Radiological Dispersion Device

Terrorist use of an RDD—often called "dirty nuke" or "dirty bomb"—is considered far more likely than use of a nuclear explosive device. An RDD combines a conventional explosive device—such as a bomb—with radioactive material. It is designed to scatter dangerous and sub-lethal amounts of radioactive material over a general area. Such RDDs appeal to terrorists because they require limited technical knowledge to build and deploy compared to a nuclear device. Also, the radioactive materials in RDDs are widely used in medicine, agriculture, industry, and research, and are easier to obtain than weapons grade uranium or plutonium.

The primary purpose of terrorist use of an RDD is to cause psychological fear and economic disruption. Some devices could cause fatalities from exposure to radioactive materials. Depending on the speed at which the area of the RDD detonation was evacuated or how successful people were at sheltering-in-place, the number of deaths and injuries from an RDD might not be substantially greater than from a conventional bomb explosion.

The size of the affected area and the level of destruction caused by an RDD would depend on the sophistication and size of the conventional bomb, the type of radioactive material used, the quality and quantity of the radioactive material, and the local meteorological conditions—primarily wind and precipitation. The area affected could be placed off-limits to the public for several months during cleanup efforts.

Before a Radiological Dispersion Device Event

There is no way of knowing how much warning time there will be before an attack by terrorists using a Radiological Dispersion Device (RDD), so being prepared in advance and knowing what to do, and when, is important.

To prepare for an RDD event, you should do the following:

- Find out from officials if any public buildings in your community have been designated as fallout shelters. If none have been designated, make your own list of potential shelters near your home, workplace, and school. These places would include basements or the windowless center area of middle floors in high-rise buildings, as well as subways and tunnels.

- If you live in an apartment building or high-rise, talk to the manager about the safest place in the building for sheltering and about providing for building occupants until it is safe to go out.

- During periods of increased threat increase your disaster supplies to be adequate for up to two weeks.

Taking shelter during an RDD event is absolutely necessary. There are two kinds of shelters - blast and fallout. The following describes the two kinds of shelters:

- **Blast shelters** are specifically constructed to offer some protection against blast pressure, initial radiation, heat, and fire. But even a blast shelter cannot withstand a direct hit from a nuclear explosion.

- **Fallout shelters** do not need to be specially constructed for protecting against fallout. They can be any protected space, provided that the walls and roof are thick and dense enough to absorb the radiation given off by fallout particles

During a Radiological Dispersion Device Event

While the explosive blast will be immediately obvious, the presence of radiation will not be known until trained personnel with specialized equipment are on the scene. Whether you are indoors or outdoors, home or at work, be extra cautious. It would be safer to assume radiological contamination has occurred—particularly in an urban setting or near other likely terrorist targets—and take the proper precautions. As with any radiation, you want to avoid or limit exposure. This is particularly true of inhaling radioactive dust that results from the explosion. As you seek shelter from any location (indoors or outdoors) and there is visual dust or other contaminants in the air, breathe through the cloth of your shirt or coat to limit your exposure. If you manage to avoid breathing radioactive dust, your proximity to the radioactive particles may still result in some radiation exposure.

If the explosion or radiological release occurs inside, get out immediately and seek safe shelter. Otherwise, if you are:

Outdoors	Indoors
Seek shelter indoors immediately in the nearest undamaged building. If appropriate shelter is not available, move as rapidly as is safe upwind and away from the location of the explosive blast. Then, seek appropriate shelter as soon as possible. Listen for official instructions and follow directions.	If you have time, turn off ventilation and heating systems, close windows, vents, fireplace dampers, exhaust fans, and clothes dryer vents. Retrieve your disaster supplies kit and a battery-powered radio and take them to your shelter room. Seek shelter immediately, preferably underground or in an interior room of a building, placing as much distance and dense shielding as possible between you and the outdoors where the radioactive material may be. Seal windows and external doors that do not fit snugly with duct tape to reduce infiltration of radioactive particles. Plastic sheeting

<table>
<tr><td></td><td>will not provide shielding from radioactivity nor from blast effects of a nearby explosion.
Listen for official instructions and follow directions</td></tr>
</table>

After a Radiological Dispersion Device (RDD) Event

After finding safe shelter, those who may have been exposed to radioactive material should decontaminate themselves. To do this, remove and bag your clothing (and isolate the bag away from you and others), and shower thoroughly with soap and water. Seek medical attention after officials indicate it is safe to leave shelter.

Contamination from an RDD event could affect a wide area, depending on the amount of conventional explosives used, the quantity and type of radioactive material released, and meteorological conditions. Thus, radiation dissipation rates vary, but radiation from an RDD will likely take longer to dissipate due to a potentially larger localized concentration of radioactive material.

Follow these additional guidelines after an RDD event:

- Continue listening to your radio or watch the television for instructions from local officials, whether you have evacuated or sheltered-in-place.

- Do not return to or visit an RDD incident location for any reason.

Nuclear Blast

A nuclear blast is an explosion with intense light and heat, a damaging pressure wave, and widespread radioactive material that can contaminate the air, water, and ground surfaces for miles around. A nuclear device can range from a weapon carried by an intercontinental missile launched by a hostile nation or terrorist organization, to a small portable nuclear device transported by an individual. All nuclear devices cause deadly effects when exploded, including blinding light, intense heat (thermal radiation), initial nuclear radiation, blast, fires started by the heat pulse, and secondary fires caused by the destruction.

Hazards of Nuclear Devices

The extent, nature, and arrival time of these hazards are difficult to predict. The geographical dispersion of hazard effects will be defined by the following:

- Size of the device. A more powerful bomb will produce more distant effects.

- Height above the ground the device was detonated. This will determine the extent of blast effects.

- Nature of the surface beneath the explosion. Some materials are more likely to become radioactive and airborne than others. Flat areas are more susceptible to blast effects.

- Existing meteorological conditions. Wind speed and direction will affect arrival time of fallout; precipitation may wash fallout from the atmosphere.

Radioactive Fallout

Even if individuals are not close enough to the nuclear blast to be affected by the direct impacts, they may be affected by radioactive fallout. Any nuclear blast results in some fallout. Blasts that occur near the earth's surface create much greater amounts of fallout than blasts that occur at higher altitudes. This is because the tremendous heat produced from a nuclear blast causes an updraft of air that forms the familiar mushroom cloud. When a blast occurs near the earth's surface, millions of vaporized dirt particles also are drawn into the cloud. As the heat diminishes, radioactive materials that have vaporized condense on the particles and fall back to Earth. The phenomenon is called radioactive fallout. This fallout material decays over a long period of time, and is the main source of residual nuclear radiation.

Fallout from a nuclear explosion may be carried by wind currents for hundreds of miles if the right conditions exist. Effects from even a small portable device exploded at ground level can be potentially deadly.

Nuclear radiation cannot be seen, smelled, or otherwise detected by normal senses. Radiation can only be detected by radiation monitoring devices. This makes radiological emergencies different from other types of emergencies, such as floods or hurricanes. Monitoring can project the fallout arrival times, which will be announced through official warning channels. However, any increase in surface buildup of gritty dust and dirt should be a warning for taking protective measures.

Radioactive Fallout

In addition to other effects, a nuclear weapon detonated in or above the earth's atmosphere can create an electromagnetic pulse (EMP), a high-density electrical field. An EMP acts like a stroke of lightning but is stronger, faster, and shorter. An EMP can seriously damage electronic devices connected to power sources or antennas. This includes communication systems, computers, electrical appliances, and automobile or aircraft ignition systems. The damage could range from a minor interruption to actual burnout of components. Most electronic equipment within 1,000 miles of a high-altitude nuclear detonation could be affected. Battery-powered radios with short antennas generally would not be affected. Although an EMP is unlikely to harm most people, it could harm those with pacemakers or other implanted electronic devices.

Protection from a Nuclear Blast

The danger of a massive strategic nuclear attack on the United States is predicted by experts to be less likely today. However, terrorism, by nature, is unpredictable.

If there were a threat of an attack, people living near potential targets could be advised to evacuate or they could decide on their own to evacuate to an area not considered a likely target. Protection from radioactive fallout would require taking shelter in an underground area or in the middle of a large building.

In general, potential targets include:

- Strategic missile sites and military bases.

- Centers of government such as Washington, DC, and state capitals.

- Important transportation and communication centers.

- Manufacturing, industrial, technology, and financial centers.

- Petroleum refineries, electrical power plants, and chemical plants.

- Major ports and airfields.

The three factors for protecting oneself from radiation and fallout are distance, shielding, and time.

- **Distance** - the more distance between you and the fallout particles, the better. An underground area such as a home or office building basement offers more protection than the first floor of a building. A floor near the middle of a high-rise may be better, depending on what is nearby at that level on which significant fallout particles would collect. Flat roofs collect fallout particles so the top floor is not a good choice, nor is a floor adjacent to a neighboring flat roof.

- **Shielding** - the heavier and denser the materials - thick walls, concrete, bricks, books and earth - between you and the fallout particles, the better.

- **Time** - fallout radiation loses its intensity fairly rapidly. In time, you will be able to leave the fallout shelter. Radioactive fallout poses the greatest threat to people during the first two weeks, by which time it has declined to about 1 percent of its initial radiation level.

Remember that any protection, however temporary, is better than none at all, and the more shielding, distance, and time you can take advantage of, the better.

To prepare for a nuclear blast, you should do the following:

- Find out from officials if any public buildings in your community have been designated as fallout shelters. If none have been designated, make your own list of potential shelters near your home, workplace, and school. These places would include basements or the windowless center area of middle floors in high-rise buildings, as well as subways and tunnels.

- If you live in an apartment building or high-rise, talk to the manager about the safest place in the building for sheltering and about providing for building occupants until it is safe to go out.

- During periods of increased threat increase your disaster supplies to be adequate for up to two weeks.

Taking shelter during a nuclear blast is absolutely necessary. There are two kinds of shelters - blast and fallout. The following describes the two kinds of shelters:

- **Blast shelters** are specifically constructed to offer some protection against blast pressure, initial radiation, heat, and fire. But even a blast shelter cannot withstand a direct hit from a nuclear explosion.

- **Fallout shelters** do not need to be specially constructed for protecting against fallout. They can be any protected space, provided that the walls and roof are thick and dense enough to absorb the radiation given off by fallout particles.

During a Nuclear Blast

The following are guidelines for what to do in the event of a nuclear explosion.

If an attack warning is issued:

- Take cover as quickly as you can, below ground if possible, and stay there until instructed to do otherwise.

- Listen for official information and follow instructions.

If you are caught outside and unable to get inside immediately:

- Do not look at the flash or fireball - it can blind you.

- Take cover behind anything that might offer protection.

- Lie flat on the ground and cover your head. If the

explosion is some distance away, it could take 30 seconds or more for the blast wave to hit.

- Take shelter as soon as you can, even if you are many miles from ground zero where the attack occurred - radioactive fallout can be carried by the winds for hundreds of miles. Remember the three protective factors: Distance, shielding, and time.

After a Nuclear Blast

Decay rates of the radioactive fallout are the same for any size nuclear device. However, the amount of fallout will vary based on the size of the device and its proximity to the ground. Therefore, it might be necessary for those in the areas with highest radiation levels to shelter for up to a month.

The heaviest fallout would be limited to the area at or downwind from the explosion, and 80 percent of the fallout would occur during the first 24 hours.

People in most of the areas that would be affected could be allowed to come out of shelter within a few days and, if necessary, evacuate to unaffected areas.

Remember the following when returning home:

- Keep listening to the radio and television for news about what to do, where to go, and places to avoid.

- Stay away from damaged areas. Stay away from areas marked "radiation hazard" or "HAZMAT." Remember that radiation cannot be seen, smelled, or otherwise detected by human senses.

WOW! They have it all figured out don't they. When I was reading their pamphlet I couldn't help but think If a government agency feels the need to state the above facts and place a county position for someone to distribute this info to everyone, it tells you what kind of world we live in.

Also, if basic human understanding is not intelligent enough to grasp the concept of "LEAVE THE AREA " Trust me when I tell you that in a time of crisis Society as a whole will be more unprepared than prepared and will want what you have. So as the experts have stated "Get out of the area as fast as possible. Lock your doors, make sure your insurance is paid up and go to your bug out location. On a side note most homeowners/renters insurance doesn't offer "in time of war" insurance or flood, so check to see what your coverage is. Because if it is a local problem whatever the looters or vandals destroy or steal can be replaced by your insurance. But the life and limb of your family cannot.

Most of the Scenarios that FEMA has discussed above are wonderful tools to at least get you thinking about the fact that a problem may occur and facilitate a conversation on "what would you do if." That is great and should be taken seriously. Yes you should Listen to the radio for information/disinformation remember that a newscaster is paid to read lines written by someone else and whatever spin they chose to put on it. As you can see some of the items on FEMA's list are also on mine because they are common sense Items that we all should know but because we are for whatever reason not always using that common sense over time it is necessary to re-iterate those basic survivor ideas.

Most people have a junk drawer, turn that drawer into a disaster drawer. Keep items in it that you will need in an emergency. Batteries, Candles, Matches, First Aid Kit and a couple days supply of necessary medicine, include Anti-Bacterial Cream, Cold Medicine, Ibuprofen, and Stomach Medicine, Dust Masks. Children and older people are more prone to illness and it can help to have these on hand. We all buy useless stuff everytime we go to the store, why not train our brains to pick up one item each time that can be used for survival.

These simple steps can go a long way. Put it in your survival drawer, your grab and go bag or even better start a survival trunk that sits in the bottom of a closet. Put one at your bug out location and one at your home this way you have resources at hand before you leave your home in case you need to stay put for awhile and you have resources available when you get to your fortified location.

Buy an Antenna because Cable and Internet probably will not be working. There are many options to choose from, try to find one that does not draw a lot of attention. Test it at your bug out location because it may not be strong enough to pick up broadcasts. I moved to the country and was surrounded by hills and could not pick any channels up with my rabbit ears. I had to buy a special antenna that worked for that type of situation so the point is know your situation and use that to select the right one.

One of the exciting items that has become available to everyone is Drones. Did you know that you can buy a small one designed for Kids for around $30? It will be a fun toy for your kids and a great tool in a disaster.

Back before the world became digital, Radios and well let's be honest things were easier to build, repair and use. Make a fun project with your kids and create an old Radio and Power Source. Plans can easily be found online and can be used as a Science Fair Project.

STOCKPILING ITEMS AT YOUR BUG OUT/ IN LOCATION

Just based on the pandemic of 2020 we now know for a fact that people will panic buy. We all know Toilet Paper, Water, Hand Sanitazer, and Rubbing Alcohol all disappeared from shelves as fast as they could be stocked. So the need to have these items stockpiled is very important.

First and foremost log on and order Canning Lids and Cannig Jars. Vinager and Salt. Those items are alway s hard to find at harvest time. Stockpiling now will save you later. Also begin saving your Glass Jars now. Be sure to buy the variety pack of Lids to accomidate each size of Jar you have.

The Pandemic also caused people to stock up on everything else as well. We live in a on demand supply chain and Trucks could not deliver Food quick enough to meet the demand. Factories were deemed not essential and sent employees home for months until the Government decided they could return. Because of this items were not available for months so items are still hard to find.

Just imgine what would happen if we have a SHTF situation. Stockpiling now can save you later.

Each time you go to the store buy a package of Beans and Rice. Flour, Corn meal, Oats, and sugar are also important to stockpile. Look around for items that state on the package "just add water". These items will be a fast meal prep when stressful times happen. Pancake mix, Brownies, Corn Bread mix and there are several dry Soup and Rice meals as well.

You can save yourself some Cash by looking around those stores where everything is a dollar. We have a Dollar Tree in my area and you can literally get a big variety stable shelf life foods there. So if you have $20 you can start stockpiling Food right away.

While at the $1 Store pick up Dog /Cat food. Salt/Pepper Spices, Broths, Bullion and Dry Milk. You can pick up packets to flavor your water. There are also many different types of OTC medicines as well. Peanut Butter and Jelly, Crackers, Coffee, Tea, and many other drink items are all availalbe.

Don't forget to think about Cleaning Supplies and bleach. Soap, Shampoo, Tampons/Pads. Midol, Cough Mmedicine, Stomach Medicine. Antibacterial Ointment, Proxcide, and multiple other items.

Duct Tape, JB Weld, Twine, Rope, Zip Ties and Bungie cords are also items that need to be in your stockpiles. Everytime you go to the store you need to be thinking about what if this is the last time you can go to the store, Because it may very well be. If it is what will your family have to eat, repair items or do if the get sick?

You also need to think about can I cook these items if the power goes out and the water is shut off? How will I store Water in large volumes? By purchasing a few extra Gallon Jugs you can start storing water very easily. Look around the camping section of Walmart, Target and all the online retailers and find a water storage container within your Budget.

CHAPTER 5
GROWING YOUR OWN FOOD

They say an Apple a day keeps the Doctor away, do you know what else does? Growing your own food without all the hamrful chemicals that are added from large scale Farming and Preserving Food designed for the retail markets.

It is a long time consuming job that needs to be started as soon as possible. Before disaster hits, plant a nut bearing tree and a fruit bearing tree. These two trees make the difference between starvation and survival. Nuts are a good source of protein and Fruit is a great source of Vitamin C. Combine the two and you are being Vegan. But, what about the variety in your diet you ask, well this is where the hard Garden Hoe, Seeds and a few pots that you can sit on a window sill come into play.

To begin the process you can also use an Egg carton which will allow you to start the plant and let it begin before you go outside and dig up the Yard. It will also help prevent the possibility of wasting Seeds.

Try starting a few different types of Vegetables on your Window Sill and then transferring them to a raised garden to begin with and expanding from there before you bug out this way you have an idea of how long each plant takes from seed to harvest. Once you have this Idea then you can expand to larger crops and sustainability because for example one ear of corn will not feed your family but 30 will feed them for a few days. Corn can also be used to make cornmeal and breading for other vegetables.

The concept of Growing your own food is really simple: you dig a hole about the first knuckle of your thumb deep, put one seed in hole cover back over and water the plant/seed daily, don't drown it , water just enough to saturate the soil but not turn into mud. Then keep weeds away. This is the hard part because weeds can and will take over a garden in less than a week this is why weed killer is sold by the gallon. If possible try to pick some up but read the label and ensure that it is garden safe and not harmful to you and what you are planting.

A few simple natural Weed killers are listed below :

1. regular table salt Using a ratio of three parts salt to one part water, dilute the salt until it's thoroughly dissolved, and pour it directly on the weeds you want gone. Be incredibly careful where you pour, especially if the weeds

are close to plants you want to keep alive. Too much sodium can damage the root structure of surrounding plants.

2. Vinegar put in a spray bottle and spray weed. Simple but effective.
3. Use newspaper to surround your plant and cover it with rocks or mulch.
4. Pick up garden screens they come in rolls of 25 ft by 3ft and cut a small hole in it for each plant.
5. Walk the garden daily and pull weeds.
6. Sprinkle cornmeal around plants

Another problem is keeping plants watered: here are some Ideals I have collected from friends and family over the years.

1. Keeping plants adequately hydrated throughout the dog days of summer is virtually a full time job. That's where this trick comes in handy. Designed to mimic a drip irrigation system, it delivers water straight to plant roots using nothing more than a plastic bottle and a sock. Puncture holes around the sides, then stuff a sock in it—the fabric will absorb and retain the water, slowly distributing it to plants. Unscrew the cap and fill the bottle when you're ready to water.
2. Keep some Miracle growth, Peat moss and Compost around to keep moisture in.

Use Screening on bottom to keep Moles out and fenced in Garden to keep critters out. Sprinkle Human hair around garden animals don't like the smell of humans.

Pick some Concrete Blocks to use as well for a raised

Garden.

A great way to grow Tomatoes is get a large Fower Pot, potting soil, wire fencing to make a tower, a small corrugated pipe a brown tarp and seeds.

Follow these steps

1. Grab the flower pot and place the fence in a circle inside the flower pot,
2. Grab the Corrugated pipe tape one end with duct tape.
3. Put pipe in the center of pot
4. Cut tarp to fit flowerpot and fence tower add potting soil around pipe
5. Poke holes in tarp and plant seeds. Plant starts work better.

Follow these Five simple steps to growing food in a small area. The pipe allows you to only need water every 2-3 days it also keeps weeds away and will allow it to be moved if necessary.

Start a grapevine at your bug out location, build an Arbor and begin as soon as possible because you can use Grapes to make Wine, Jelly, Jam, Raisins, Vinegar, and as a sweet treat for Children. Grape Leaves can be used to stop Bleeding, reduce Inflammation, and pain.

CHAPTER 6: CANNING, WATER, FOOD PRESERVATION
Making water Potable(drinkable)

rule 1 Always boil your Water.

Let's start with Water because Humans cannot survive without it and it will be needed for everything from drinking to growing Food and staying clean. Rain Water is a great way to collect and store Water for future use but is also a breeding ground for mosquitoes so if possible plant some citronella plants near rain barrels. If you don't have rain barrels you can use plastic totes Trash Cans, Basically anything that can hold water including a blow up Swimming Pool.

Water must be Potable (drinkable) therefore you need to be able to make it safe. There are several ways to accomplish this; using water purifying tablets, Filtration, and Boiling. Regardless of which method you use, be sure to strain your water as many times as possible before using any of the below techniques.

1. Water purifying tablets: simply Drop in water and wait the amount of time indicated on the bottle.
2. Boling is another simple way to purify water simply boil water for 5 minutes then pour into a container and let cool.
3. Filtration can be a little more complex

A, Find a piece of Tree Bark (Birch works best because it holds its shape)

B. Form it into the shape of a cone

C. Layer it with Stones, Grass, Charcoal Sand.

D. Pour Water through the cone several times. Each time will remove additional impurities but will not purify Water.

Pasteurizing Milk

The CDC says that consuming unpasteurized milk causes increased risk to bacterial infection. More Importantly in a SHTF situation you can not risk unnecessary exposure to infection. Pasteurizing milk is a relatively easy process if you follow these steps.

1. Strain Milk 3 times stepping down to more fine strainers
2. Pour in a clean sanitized pot
3. Heat to 162 degrees and maintain heat above for 15 seconds.
4. Remove from heat immediately.
5. Cool Milk as fast as possible the faster it cools the better it will taste.

6. It needs to reach 40 degrees so an Ice bath is rec-ommended (if a freezer is available use it besure to keep lid on and check temperature often. If the temperature has not been reached in 4 hours consider milk contaminated and repeat steps 1-5 again, understand that taste will be lost due to the repeating process.
7. Once temp has been reached, refrigerate in a sani-tized container.
8. Once this is done correctly your milk should be safe to drink for 7 days.

Canning Vegetables

The first and foremost thing to remember when canning is that if done incorrectly it can cause Botulism! That is why you cannot just wing it you must practice before there is no other option. Now I know that statement is scary but trust me you can do this. Remember people have been pre-serving foods for many centuries. We have just gotten lazy and have forgotten the old ways.

Luckily not everyone has forgotten and we can use their knowledge to relearn the old ways. When I was little My grandmother always canned and so we would help her with the process. She would always have a pot boiling on the stove or a pressure cooker ready. Once she had those prepared, then she would begin cutting her vegetables that she was going to can. It is one of my favorite memories with her. Now you can have that memory with your chil-dren and grandchildren by learning how she did it.

There are two types of canning foods those with highly acidic properties and those with low acidic properties:

High acid foods require boiling and are:

Citrus fruits, cucumbers, tomatoes,

Low acid foods require pressure and are:

Green beans, corn, Peas

The first step in canning Vegetables it to have jars to can the vegetables in these jars can be any size and any shape. But must have a sealable lid.   You don't want to spend time canning your food then find out that your lid was bad. So again prior planning prevents poor performance. Every spring/summer stores begin selling canning jars and supplies.

Buy 2 cases of canning jars and take them to your bug out location. Also buy a set to have at your home to practice canning with. Then once you have mastered canning take the food you have stored to your bug out location. So you will have food you like when you get there. This will help sustain you till you can get your garden going and will help you have additional jars for canning. Rule to use is can half of the food you grow. Use a fourth of it fresh from the garden and put the remainder aside to use as a source for seeding the next garden.

Track how much your family eats in a month, you will need that many jars times 3 because a 90 day supply should always be maintained. Remember gardens are a warm weather activity. So you will need to have food stored for the winter months. You should also plant two different varieties of Nut bearing trees. They become ripe in the fall and will help feed your family in the winter months. A Nut tree can be planted in a yard in the City or county. If possible plant a fruit tree as well.

Once you have your canning jars and are ready to begin canning these are the steps to follow.

One thing to alway have is cast iron pots and pans. There are many advantages to having these items.

1. They are durable

2. They are non stick

3. You clean them with water only no soap needed

4. You can use them over an open fire

5. They can be used at any temperature

6. They last forever.

7. They can also be used as a weapon.

8. They have been used for centuries.

9. Food tastes better when cooked in them

10. They are cheaper than most other cookware sets.

Remember there are 365 days in a year and you need to be able to feed your family on each of those days. So plan to have enough Canning Jars to accomplish that. There is no way that i can teach you to Can every type of food there is so buy a book or search the internet and print off instructions for each of the types of seeds you have. that is why I am only going to give a few common examples of canning. as always do your due dilagence and test each canning reciept for yourself before you have to rely on it for surival.

Canning whole Kernal Corn

Bear in mind that 31 pounds of Sweet Corn is needed

per 7 quarts and 20 pounds for 9 pints a bushel of Corn weighs 35 pounds and makes between 6=11 quarts. So basically 4.5 pounds per quart canned.

Always remember quality is important. select ears that are slighty immature and of high quality for a freasher taste. but if to immature it will cause browning. always test a small batch before picking a lot to can.

1. Begin by removing Husk from Stalk.

2. Remove Shell and Silk donot scrape Cob

3. Wash with Potable Water

4. Boil for 3-4 minute

5. Cut Corn from Cob at about 3/4th of the depth of the Kernel,

Using The Hot Pack Method

1. 1 Cup of Potabe Water per clean Quart of Kernels in Sausepan,

2. Heat to boiling and then reduce heat to simmer for 5 minutes

3. Add 1 Teaspoon of Salt per Quart to the Jar.

4, Fill jar with Corn and Cooking liquid.

5. leave 1 inch headspace at top of Jar.

Using The Raw Pack Method

1. Fll Jars with Raw Kernels

2. Leave 1 inch space at top of Jar.

3. Donot Shake or press down

4. Add 1 Teaspoon of Salt per quart

5. Leave 1 inch space at top of Jar

6. Add fresh Potable boiling Water

7. Leave 1 inch above Water at top of Jar

8. Seal Jar with Canning Lid

To ensure you have a Strong Seal on Jar to prevent Spoiling you can add a layer of Canning Wax to each Jar. Store in a cool dry place until needed.

REMEMBER!! ALWAYS USE POTABLE WATER FOR CANNING!

Canning Meat

Chicken or Rabbit

Choose a Healty and Fresly killed Animal. chickens once cleaned and dressed should be chilled for 6 to 12 hours befor canning them.

Rabbits should be soaked for an hour with 1 Tablespoon of Salt per quart and then rinse Rabbit, trim excess Fat, debone and cut in small sizes to fit in Jar easily and will leave some head space.

it is best to hot pack for quality preservation during storage. to do this you need to do the following steps.

1. Boil, Steam or Bake until 2/3 done.

2. Add 1 teaspoon Salt per quart to the Jar.

3. Add Meat and Juices to Jar.

4. Leave 1 1/4 inch head space at top of Jar.

5. Seal with Canning Lid,

If you can't use the hot pack method and must can it raw, follow these steps

1. Add 1 Teaspoon of Salt per quart

2. Add Meat pieces

3. Leave 1 1/4 head space at top of Jar.

4. Seal with Canning Lid

Canning Soup

Before we begin. I want to caution you that you cannot add Noodles, Pasta, Rice, Flour, Cream Milk or any other thickening methods to this process. Do ont use dehydrated foods unless they have been rehydrated before hand, start by selecting, washing, prepare each item i,e:

Vegetables, Meat according to their own canning instructions following the hot pack method for each ingredient, then salt to taste combine in jar with meat broth or water, boil for 5-6 minutes, seal with Canning Jar.

Important notice be sure to apply at least 11 pounds of pressure seal to each lid.

Again take the time you have to gather Canning instructions for as many differnt typs of food you can. As I have repeatly stated it is best to have a printed copy of everything because in a survival situation you may not be able to access digital files.

Cold Storage

Keeping food cold and fresh is a daily struggle in a bug out situation. One method is to build a Cellar that can be used to refrigerate items. People have used these for centuries the reason is because the earth has a lower temperature than the air. This can be relatively easy to accomplish but will require a certain amount of Sweat and Shovels.

Start by digging a Hole about 15 feet deep and create a Cave then put a door on it to keep out the Sunlight. Keeping out the Sun will help keep temperature low. It will also make it dark. Run a set of Solar String lights to it so you can have light when you need to enter.

There are also Battery operated Coolers and there are even Solar Refrigerators a quick Amazon search showed prices range from $30-1000. So it is affordable in every price range. There are also ones ran on Propane. Always remember you will need to have a steady supply of Propane if you go that route.

A simple method is to put a large wooden box in the ground, build a rain runoff over it and store your food in it for winter use.

> disclaimer: I am not certified in any food preservation way. these are just techniques that I was taught by my grandmother, other family members, friends, and my own trial and error.

CHAPTER 7
ALTERNATE POWER SOURCES

There are many alternate power sources out there you have Generators: Human powered, Gas, Propane, Solar, Water and Wind powered. All of which cost a lot of money to have and maintain if you want to power a modern home on a consistent daily basis. But what if you looked at smaller ones that are for charging Batteries, and powering Solar String Lights, Solar flashlights.

A 1000w Gas Generator used to quick charge a stove or small cooler. A 100w wind generator that is used to run a well pump is usually a cheaper option. These can be used to sustain the basics we need to survive. Remember with the exception of the last 100 years mankind has never had a power source so it can be done.

Again think small in the beginning. Buy some solar lights at your local store and set them in the sun to charge at your bug out location. Make sure at least one of them are Solar String lights that can be strung around the inside of your house. Another thing you should think about is what can I run off batteries(rechargeable), you can buy camping fans to help circulate air and cool down in the heat of Summer. Fans can be used to remove Cooking Smoke from your home and direct heat in Winter.

You can get Camping Stoves that run off of Propane, most stores sell little Bottles of Propane for a few Dollars. Which means they could be picked up and dropped off at bugout location each visit.

Here is an example of one by Coleman that is under $20.

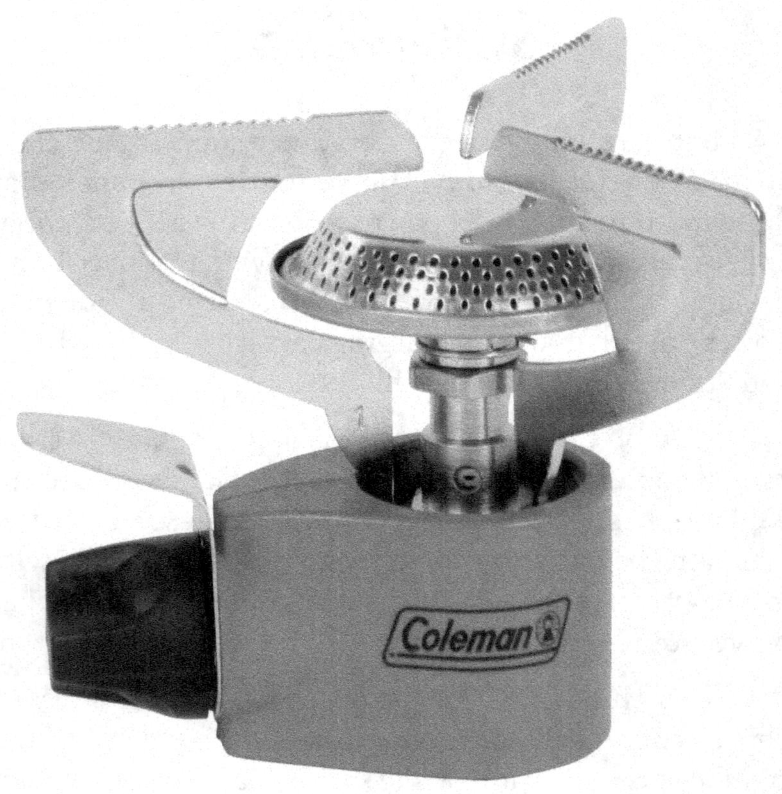

Look around your local RV supply centers and truck stops. They have all kinds of inexpensive Gadgets that are

DC powered and can be used in a bug out situation. For example they have DC powered Heaters that Truck Drivers use and can plug into a Car plug or a portable power charger most portable solar panels come with a DC and USB Port. They sell Fans to help cool and circulate air in summer and can be used to help circulate heat from a Fire in the Winter.

NAPA sells this one for under $50.

Try to buy a Deep Cycle Battery, they are designed to supply steady power for longer periods. Whereas a car battery is designed to give a large amount of power for a short period of time. As you can see Deep cycle is the best option that is why they are used in Boats, RV's Golf Carts, and with Solar Power Stations.

When it comes to lighting your home there are Solar Shed Lights that are great and put out of a good amount of light and can be purchased online for as low as $10. You set the Solar Panel outside and a long wire through window allows you to mount light inside.

Amazon has this one listed for around $40.

Walmart sells the below one for under $50

There are also DC power chargers that you can purchase that plug into you car and if you have your gas cans filled like I have suggested you can charge them using the two plug inverter, an example is pictured below:

These can be purchased at your local retailer or online for around $10. they work great for road trips as well.

CHAPTER 8 FIRST AID/ HOME REMEDIES/SAFETY

In time of crisis even the most insignificant scratch can be fatal if not cared for. By preparing in advance you can save yourself and your family a lot of pain and anguish. Buy some Antibacterial Cream and store it at your bug out location, in your Vehicle, you will need at least One Tube for each Person. If possible a Second Tube for each person at your bug out location.

It is important to take a First Aid class to learn basic Lifesaving skills. Learn how to apply a Splint. Seal a wound, treat Dysentery, Scurvy. These are just a few things that are common in SHTF situations. That is why it is very important to take care of as many possible scenarios as possible. There are many Vaccines available that stop diseases that are common in third world countries. Which is what the world will become in a SHTF situation. Typhoid, Yellow Fever, Smallpox, Polio, H1N1, Malaria, Hepatitis A & B Vaccines, Tetanus-Diphtheria Vaccine, Meningococcal Vaccine, and the Pneumonia Vaccine. For extra precaution get the shingles vaccination. Now there is a COVID-19 Vaccine.

There is a reason that Military personnel are vaccinated against these diseases on a routine basis. The Military needs to be prepared to move at a moment's notice to handle any threat that presents itself. In A SHTF so do you! There is an old saying Prior planning prevents poor performance. These are words the military lives by. They train continuously for worse case scenarios. So should you!.

I am lucky because I have spent 22 years in the Military training and training others in those scenarios, while there is no way to be prepared for everything it is possible to have enough knowledge about other scenarios that it becomes possible to navigate the unknown. Life will alway throw you a curveball when you least expect it. One moment you can be perfectly healthy and a low lying branch will trip you and cause a sprained ankle. Do you know how to treat a sprained ankle or worse a broken one?

Basic First Aid Guide:

Strains, Sprains and Broken Bones

If an injured Arm or Leg begins to swell, make a splint and tie securely using pieces of Cloth to keep from moving. You will also want to make a sling for an injured Arm.

How to make a Splint:

Rap injured area to provide stability and find a Board or Stick to place on each side be sure not to cover Bone if it is protruding. Use a Second Cloth to secure the stick to injury.

How to control Bleeding:

1. Use a wadded cloth to apply direct pressure and use a second cloth to Secure pressure dressing.
2. Elevate injured area
3. If bleeding continues apply a second pressure dressing over the first dressing.
4. Last resort is to use a tourniquet.
    - Use a stick and cloth to stop blood flow at the pressure point above wound by rapping cloth above wound and using stick to tighten cloth one quarter turn at a time until blood slows to a trickle. (do not use it for head or neck wounds).
    - Pressure points are located on the human body at Temple, Jaw, neck, collar bone, inner upper arm, inner elbow, wrist, upper thigh, groin, knee, and ankle.

ABC's of CPR

1. Open Airway-check for breathing
2. Two breaths
3. 30 compressions

When it comes to performing CPR I would recommend you take a Class because it is very important that you understand how to do the compressions correctly. But it is explained in its simplest form below.

First begin by pinching Nose closed, tilting Head back and lifting Chin to open the Airway then check for any obstruction in the Airway, make a finger into a hook and gently sweep open Mouth to remove any choking hazard. Then with nose pinches and head tilted and neck supported Blow two quick breaths while watching to ensure the chest is rising and then give 30 compressions trace the line of Ribs and compress just below in the center press downward approximately two inches each compression. (Again take a class because if done incorrectly this could cause broken Ribs if not done correctly.) be sure to check for a pulse after each round of breaths and compressions.

This is a great time to talk about Duct Tape and its uses in Frst Aide. Here are six practical uses.

1. You can remove a wart by covering it in duct tape. Apply a fresh piece of duct tape everyday for 6 days then soak in warm water on the seventh day and then scrub with emery board.
2. Fold a piece of duct tape in half so it sticks together and you can use it to perform CPR
3. cut small strips of duct tape and use as a butterfly bandage to close a wound.
4. Use it with gauze to protect blisters.
5. Create a sling for a injured limb
6. Create waterproof shoes if you need to walk through contaminated water.

BURNS

1st & 2nd Degree:

Skin turns Red & possible Blisters

TREATMENT

Immediately cool the burned area in cool Water until there is little to no pain. Pat dry & cover with a moist dressing & bandage loosely. Change dressing every 4 hours and keep the area clean. DON'T BREAK THE BLISTERS!! DON'T USE OINTMENTS, CREAMS OR SPRAYS!!

Disclaimer I am not a Medical provider/ doctor so seek medical advice from actual medical providers/doctors. the information in this book is just knowledge that a have aquired through my Army training and my own personal mishaps and searching various trial and error methods.

CHAPTER 9
PREPARING/ NOT SCARING CHILDREN

Children are wonderful, caring, loving, and inexperienced in the events that shape our lives. Their view of the world is controlled by what we parents allow them to see. This is a wonderful job that should not be taken lightly. We need to teach our Children to be respectable, responsible, productive members of society. How this is accomplished is slowly introducing them to how messed up the World is and teaching them how to be a good person. As we adults know the World is not full of people that have our best interest at heart and will in many cases, kill you for the .50 cents you may have.

Children must from an early age be taught to understand that bad things happen. No matter how good you live your life someone is simultaneously living their life to make yours difficult. Be it shoddy craftsmanship that causes a Building to collapse, Levee break, a bunch of rioters bent on destruction, a country deciding that we do not like your country, a madman with a gun in an airport, or simply a car crash on a back road. Each of these cases cause children stress and will send them into a terrified panic. There are ways to lessen this panic. By giving them the tools to understand to help out and what steps to take if they need to take control.

Here are some Ideas of non scary ways to get them thinking about the possibility of "bad things" Be prepared for so really funny responses in the beginning.

1. Make a game of what would you do "IF" .
2. Spend a day teaching them about safety in public.
3. Tell them about bad things that are happening around them.
4. Don't hide the horrors of the world from your children
5. Prepare them by talking to them in advance
6. explain that bad things happen even to good people.

More from FEMA

Disasters can leave children feeling frightened, confused, and insecure. Whether a child has personally experienced trauma, has merely seen the event on television, or has heard it discussed by adults, it is important for parents and teachers to be informed and ready to help if reactions to stress begin to occur.

Children may respond to disaster by demonstrating fears, sadness, or behavioral problems. Younger children may return to earlier behavior patterns, such as bedwetting, sleep problems, and separation anxiety. Older children may also display anger, aggression, school problems, or withdrawal. Some children who have only indirect contact with the disaster but witness it on television may develop distress.

Who is at Risk?

For many children, reactions to disasters are brief and represent normal reactions to "abnormal events." A smaller number of children can be at risk for more enduring psychological distress as a function of three major risk factors:

- Direct exposure to the disaster, such as being evacuated, observing injuries or death of others, or experiencing injury along with fearing one's life is in danger.

- Loss/grief: This relates to the death or serious injury of family or friends.

- On-going stress from the secondary effects of disaster, such as temporarily living elsewhere, loss of friends and social networks, loss of personal property, parental unemployment, and costs incurred during recovery to return the family to pre-disaster life and living conditions.

What Creates Vulnerabilities in Children?

In most cases, depending on the risk factors above, distressing responses are temporary. In the absence of severe threat to life, injury, loss of loved ones, or secondary problems such as loss of home, movies, etc., symptoms usually diminish over time. For those that were directly exposed to the disaster, reminders of the disaster such as high winds, smoke, cloudy skies, sirens, or other reminders of the disaster may cause upsetting feelings to return. Having a prior history of some type of traumatic event or severe stress may contribute to these feelings.

Children's coping with disaster or emergencies is often tied to the way parents cope. They can detect adults' fears and sadness. Parents and adults can make disasters less traumatic for children by taking steps to manage their own feelings and plans for coping. Parents are almost always the best source of support for children in disasters. One way to establish a sense of control and to build confidence in children before a disaster is to engage and involve them in preparing a family disaster plan. After a disaster, children can contribute to a family recovery plan.

A Child's Reaction to Disaster by Age

Below are common reactions in children after a disaster or traumatic event.

Birth through 2 years. When children are pre-verbal and experience a trauma, they do not have the words to describe the event or their feelings. However, they can retain memories of particular sights, sounds, or smells. Infants may react to trauma by being irritable, crying more than usual, or wanting to be held and cuddled. The biggest influence on children of this age is how their parents cope. As children get older, their play may involve acting out elements of the traumatic event that occurred several years in the past and was seemingly forgotten.

Preschool - 3 through 6 years. Preschool children often feel helpless and powerless in the face of an overwhelming event. Because of their age and small size, they lack the ability to protect themselves or others. As a result, they feel intense fear and insecurity about being separated from caregivers. Preschoolers cannot grasp the concept of permanent loss. They can see consequences as being reversible or permanent. In the weeks following a traumatic event, preschoolers play activities may reenact the incident or the disaster over and over again.

School age - 7 through 10 years. The school-age child has the ability to understand the permanence of loss. Some children become intensely preoccupied with the details of a traumatic event and want to talk about it continually. This preoccupation can interfere with the child's concentration at school and academic performance may decline. At school, children may hear inaccurate information from peers. They may display a wide range of reactions—sadness, generalized fear, or specific fears of the disaster happening again, guilt over action or inaction during the disaster, anger that the event was not prevented, or fantasies of playing rescuer.

Pre-adolescence to adolescence - 11 through 18 years. As children grow older, they develop a more sophisticated understanding of the disaster event. Their responses are more similar to adults. Teenagers may become involved in dangerous, risk-taking behaviors, such as reckless driving, or alcohol or drug use. Others can become fearful of leaving home and avoid previous levels of activities. Much of adolescence is focused on moving out into the world. After a trauma, the view of the world can seem more dangerous and unsafe. A teenager may feel overwhelmed by intense emotions and yet feel unable to discuss them with others.

Meeting the Child's Emotional Needs

Children's reactions are influenced by the behavior, thoughts, and feelings of adults. Adults should encourage children and adolescents to share their thoughts and feelings about the incident. Clarify misunderstandings about risk and danger by listening to children's concerns and answering questions. Maintain a sense of calm by validating children's concerns and perceptions and with discussion of concrete plans for safety.

Listen to what the child is saying. If a young child

is asking questions about the event, answer them simply without the elaboration needed for an older child or adult. Some children are comforted by knowing more or less information than others; decide what level of information your particular child needs. If a child has difficulty expressing feelings, allow the child to draw a picture or tell a story of what happened.

Try to understand what is causing anxieties and fears. Be aware that following a disaster, children are most afraid that:

- The event will happen again.

- Someone close to them will be killed or injured.

- They will be left alone or separated from the family.

Reassuring Children After a Disaster

Suggestions to help reassure children include the following:

- Personal contact is reassuring. Hug and touch your children.

- Calmly provide factual information about the recent disaster and current plans for ensuring their safety along with recovery plans.

- Encourage your children to talk about their feelings.

- Spend extra time with your children such as at bedtime.

- Re-establish your daily routine for work, school, play, meals, and rest.

- Involve your children by giving them specific chores to help them feel they are helping to restore family and community life.

- Praise and recognize responsible behavior.

- Understand that your children will have a range of reactions to disasters.
- Encourage your children to help update your family disaster plan.

If you have tried to create a reassuring environment by following the steps above, but your child continues to exhibit stress, if the reactions worsen over time, or if they cause interference with daily behavior at school, at home, or with other relationships, it may be appropriate to talk to a professional. You can get professional help from the child's primary care physician, a mental health provider specializing in children's needs, or a member of the clergy.

Monitor and Limit Your Family's Exposure to the Media

News coverage related to a disaster may elicit fear and confusion and arouse anxiety in children. This is particularly true for large-scale disasters or a terrorist event where significant property damage and loss of life has occurred. Particularly for younger children, repeated images of an event may cause them to believe the event is recurring over and over.

If parents allow children to watch television or use the Internet where images or news about the disaster are shown, parents should be with them to encourage communication and provide explanations. This may also include parent's monitoring and appropriately limiting their own exposure to anxiety-provoking information.

Use Support Networks

Parents help their children when they take steps to understand and manage their own feelings and ways of coping. They can do this by building and using social support systems of family, friends, community organizations and agencies, faith-based institutions, or other resources that work for that family. Parents can build their own unique social support systems so that in an emergency situation or when a disaster strikes, they can be supported and helped to manage their reactions. As a result, parents will be more available to their children and better able to support them. Parents are almost always the best source of support for children in difficult times. But to support their children, parents need to attend to their own needs and have a plan for their own support.

Preparing for disaster helps everyone in the family accept the fact that disasters do happen, and provides an opportunity to identify and collect the resources needed to meet basic needs after disaster. Preparation helps; when people feel prepared, they cope better and so do children

The emotional toll that disaster brings can sometimes be even more devastating than the financial strains of damage and loss of home, business, or personal property.

Understand Disaster Events

- Everyone who sees or experiences a disaster is affected by it in some way.
- It is normal to feel anxious about your own safety and that of your family and close friends.
- Profound sadness, grief, and anger are normal reactions to an abnormal event.
- Acknowledging your feelings helps you recover.
- Focusing on your strengths and abilities helps you heal.
- Accepting help from community programs and resources is healthy.
- Everyone has different needs and different ways of

coping.

- It is common to want to strike back at people who have caused great pain.

Children and older adults are of special concern in the aftermath of disasters. Even individuals who experience a disaster "second hand" through exposure to extensive media coverage can be affected.

Contact local faith-based organizations, voluntary agencies, or professional counselors for counseling. Additionally, FEMA and state and local governments of the affected area may provide crisis counseling assistance.

Recognize Signs of Disaster Related Stress

When adults have the following signs, they might need crisis counseling or stress management assistance:

- Difficulty communicating thoughts.
- Difficulty sleeping.
- Difficulty maintaining balance in their lives.
- Low threshold of frustration.
- Increased use of drugs/alcohol.
- Limited attention span.
- Poor work performance.
- Headaches/stomach problems.
- Tunnel vision/muffled hearing.
- Colds or flu-like symptoms.
- Disorientation or confusion.
- Difficulty concentrating.
- Reluctance to leave home.
- Depression, sadness.
- Feelings of hopelessness.

- Mood-swings and easy bouts of crying.
- Overwhelming guilt and self-doubt.
- Fear of crowds, strangers, or being alone.

Easing Disaster-Related Stress

The following are ways to ease disaster-related stress:

- Talk with someone about your feelings - anger, sorrow, and other emotions - even though it may be difficult.
- Seek help from professional counselors who deal with post-disaster stress.
- Do not hold yourself responsible for the disastrous event or be frustrated because you feel you cannot help directly in the rescue work.
- Take steps to promote your own physical and emotional healing by healthy eating, rest, exercise, relaxation, and meditation.
- Maintain a normal family and daily routine, limiting demanding responsibilities on yourself and your family.
- Spend time with family and friends.
- Participate in memorials.
- Use existing support groups of family, friends, and religious institutions.
- Ensure you are ready for future events by restocking your disaster supplies kits and updating your family disaster plan. Doing these positive actions can be comforting.

CHAPTER 10 I HAVEN'T PREPARED AT ALL

Life is what happens while we are busy making plans- anonymous fact of life

OH no I have read the book but haven't prepared at all! What do I do now? First take a deep calming breath and look around. You have more than you think you do. After-all you live everyday surviving in normal society. Lets go through a few Scenarios.

Scenario 1.

You wake up and find you can hardly breath because smoke is coming through your windows and doors. There is a Forest Fire and you have to move quickly. First ,You scream for everyone to get up, tell them to grab Clothes Shoes and run to the front Door. While everyone is running from Bedrooms, go to the Kitchen and grab whatever you have to Eat/Drink on the run, grab Purse/Wallet, Cell Phone, damp Towels for each Person and leave as fast as possible.

If possible grab, one Toy for each Child (even better Idea is to always keep some Toys and a change of Clothes/ Diapers Baby Bottles in each Vehicle, why don't you do that right now) and this book for you. Don't forget your pets!!!! Be sure to get some food and water for them as well. Don't forget their leash (if possible just keep an extra on in the glove box. If you have an extra one go put in the car now).

Some Blankets would be a smart grab as well in case you need to sleep in the Car. Move to the furthest point you can from the affected area. Always remember the further away from the problem you are the easier it will be to find accommodations and resources. Listen to Radio and follow Evacuation instructions. Once you are safely away, update Social Media/Family that you are safe.

Scenario 2.

There has been an incident that has caused a lot of Civil unrest in your area. But you can't leave the area. Tape Windows in case Bricks or other Projectiles are being thrown through Windows. Board them up if possible. By moving large items in front of Windows and Doors you can prevent those that are participating in the Civil unrest easily entering your home.

Try to stay away from the visible areas of your home. Have a Weapon ready in case these insurgents breach your home. Find a room that you can hide and wait it out bring Food and Drinks into the room and make it as comfortable as possible. You may want to have earbuds for family members so the can watch movies, play games without making noise.

Besure to turn out lights and if possible completely cover Window area so no light or shadow can be seen from outside understand that the Police and Frst Responders will be busy and will not be able to help you quickly. So be prepared to Stand Your Ground defending your Family and if necessary put out your own Fires via Fre Extinguishers or Buckets of Water (remember your Washing Maching Hose can be used to fill buckets quickly.

Scenario 3

You have lost your job and you only have one week before you are ejected from your home and are broke. During that week look around your house and find what you can live without list those items on Social Media for quick sale and put that Money back until you have enough to get a small Storage Unit. You can usually rent a unit in a small Town cheaper than in a City. Move stuff into Storage and set it up as if you live there.

No you cant live there! but you can visit it for extended periods of time under the pretense of organizing it. Most storage facilities have an overhead light this can be adapted to be a plugin by purchasing a light bulb socket with plugins on side. You can plug in a Electric Skillet, Crockpot or Recharge Electronics for use later. In the Winter you can plug in a Space Heater to keep warm while preparing Food or Kids take a Nap.

Best case is you can use it daily if you don't make a spectacle of yourself and draw attention to yourself. If someone asks why you are there so much say you buy and sell stuff on line and you need to be in and out a-lot to pick up items, organize, conduct inventory control and add new items to your inventory. Try to stage storage unit so the person asking cannot see you living area. Make it look like it is full of boxes. Keep an empty tub for bathing near the back. Also most parks have restrooms and can be a place to fill water bottles for use later.

You can rent a PO Box at the post office to receive mail and ensure that you receive important documents. When filling out applications you can use that as your address. Don't forget to put in a forwarding address. Libraries are a great place to sit for extended periods. It is not unusual for people to bring their families in to read, get on the computer and search for jobs.

They have activities that the children can participate in as well. Again don't do this each day all day. While you are adapting to you new reality of homelessness use this time to look for areas that you can stay in cheaply i.e camp grounds, extended family, friends, there are some hotels that have weekly rates.

When staying with family and friends, always remember you are a guest so don't wear out your welcome and make sure they see that you are making every effort to leave as quick as possible and even if that means taking a job that is minimum wage. Evan a minimum wage job will pay your storage fee and buy some food and gas for your car. It may even pay for a weekly rental at hotel or campground.

Always remember just because you are in this situation now one day you will be back into a regular home and stay positive. Always be looking for a better job and better living arrangement. Stay vigilant and alway try to keep a change jar going to save a little for emergencies because there will always be emergencies.

Scenario 4

There is a Foreign Power/Civil WAR that has invaded your

area and War has arrived at your door step try to remain calm and wait for the active Battle to pass if you can leave the area grab as much Food, Water, Clothing, valuables and identity paperwork as possible. Lock up your home and hope that you can return soon.   But be prepared for an extended stay somewhere else or returning to a home that may no longer be livable or may not have working utilities. Stores may be closed or destroyed and may have been looted.

So if possible acquire as much of life's necessities before returning to area. Understand that everyone else will be doing this as well. So be prepared to pay more or fight for what you need. Look for a way to acquire the items listed in the first chapter and prepare to bug in for the duration of hostilities. Make your self useful to the friendly forces they will have the resources you need and will help you stay safe.

CHAPTER 11
CONCLUSION

The reality of any disaster or collapse is that no matter how prepared you think you are, you will still find yourself unprepared for the collapse or disaster. We are told in the Military that no plans survive engagement with the enemy because they have their own plan. So does mother nature. Always understand that.But, at the same time it is better to have a plan than to just wing it.

That is what this book is about offering ideas and suggestions to get you started with your plans to survive whatever this life throws at you. Take care of you and your family. As you read through my suggestions I am sure you came up with your own thoughts on what is needed to survive the collapse of society. That is great because everyone has different needs and different ideas of what is important to them and those they love.

Some of you will even use this as a guide to make the situation worse for those that have prepared. I hope that is not the case, because we will need each other to rebuild and return our world to some semblance of a working society that promotes the common good. As the saying goes, United we stand, Divided we fall.

This book is not designed to give you all the answers but is designed to get you a few idea's that can get you in the mindset that you need to start now and save your self a lot of stress later. Alway pick up somthing extra every-time you go to the store. Visit the camping section and pick up someting from there as well.

Propane Tanks are very important in a SHTF reality make them a priority. A Camping stove that can be used with them to cook and for heat in the winter is import-ant, and a fan in the summer can keep tempatures tolerble. Food, Water and Medicine are items you and your pets can not live without. Keep your pets safe as well because they may save your life in a crisis.

Always be planning and thinking how can I protect and keep those I love safe and healty. In closing I honestly hope that you never have a need to use any information that you have read in the guide. Stay safe and away be pre-pared and watch for my next book in this series.

www.ingramcontent.com/pod-product-compliance
Lightning Source LLC
Chambersburg PA
CBHW070749250726
48662CB00004B/1709